TRAI

ATHENEUM BOOKS FOR YOUNG READERS
NEW YORK   LONDON   TORONTO   SYDNEY

N S

L Y N N   C U R L E E

ALL ABOARD!

My hometown exists because of the railroad. I grew up in High Point, North Carolina, a small southern city of factories, churches, and quiet residential neighborhoods. Today nearly one hundred thousand people live there, but a century and a half ago, before the trains came, there was no town at all—only a few farms, a sawmill, and a couple of inns where stagecoaches stopped. When the surveyors for the North Carolina Railroad arrived in 1855 and pitched their tents, Captain Gregg, the chief engineer, proclaimed, "Boys, this is the highest point along the entire line, so we will drive a stake here and call it High Point." And so the tiny settlement was actually named by the railroad.

A few months later, after the track had been laid, the first train arrived, and people came in their horse-drawn carriages and farm wagons from miles around to see a locomotive. They must have been absolutely amazed. According to town lore, as the train came into view, the engineer playfully lashed the machine with a stagecoach whip. When the train stopped, he asked the ladies in the crowd to lower their parasols so as not to startle the "iron horse," and that's just what they did, giving everyone a good laugh!

At first High Point was merely a train crossing, but by the beginning of the Civil War in 1861, it was home to around five hundred people. And in the decades after the war was over, the population exploded as enterprising men built furniture and textile factories and started other businesses near the railroad stop. By the turn of the twentieth century, modest fortunes were being made by the owners of these thriving businesses—fortunes made possible by the railroad, the lifeline of commerce that connected the growing little town to the rest of the world. The new century also brought a new invention—the automobile. Because of increasing traffic, a railroad underpass through town was built in the late 1930s. The tracks were lowered into a huge trench, with bridges for cross-streets so that cars no longer had to stop for the trains.

When I was a small boy in the 1950s, the railroad had been around for a century. By then High Point had a population of about fifty thousand people, and was home to much of the nation's furniture industry. The train depot occupied the exact center of town, where the tracks crossed under Main Street, once the old stagecoach road. Sometimes my dad took me to the station to watch the trains come through. Most of them were freight trains—looming black steam locomotives with exposed machinery, pumping rods, and massive wheels pulling dingy boxcars. As they chugged through town, the big engines belched smoke and hissed billowing clouds of steam that filled the air like dense, warm, musky fog. But my favorite was the Crescent, the luxury passenger train that ran all the way from New York City to New Orleans, right through the heart of our sleepy little southern city. Its gleaming stainless-steel cars were pulled by big, sleek, green-and-gold diesel locomotives that hummed and throbbed with power.

My grandparents lived about a mile from the railroad station in a rambling old house. Sometimes when the entire family gathered there for holidays, we would all stay over. My cousins and I slept in one big bed in an ice-cold upstairs room, warm and snug under a thick pile of heavy quilts. If the wind was blowing just right, we could hear and almost feel the trains rumbling through town. We listened to the rhythmic *clickety-clack* of their steel wheels against the rails and the plaintive echoes of their whistles dying away as the trains sped through the night. Where were they going? What would we find if we went there too?

THE IRON HORSE

Today it is hard to imagine, but before railroads, just two centuries ago, there were only three ways to travel on land. You could walk, ride an animal, or be carried in a vehicle pulled by animals. Since travel was slow, difficult, and expensive, most people never ventured far from the place where they were born. Society was based upon land and agriculture, and literally everything produced by human beings was made by hand. But in the late 1700s, for the first time in history, people began to develop and use machines for manufacturing goods and doing work. This important movement began in England and is known today as the Industrial Revolution.

One key invention was the steam engine. Its basic principle is very simple—when water is boiled and converted to steam, it expands more than one thousand times in volume. In a steam engine, water contained inside an enclosed boiler is heated by a fire. As the water boils, the expanding steam is forced into a hollow cylinder fitted inside with a sliding piston. The pressure of the steam drives the piston back and forth in the cylinder, and this movement provides power for tasks such as pumping water, running a loom, or turning a wheel. Several Englishmen experimented with steam engines during the eighteenth century, but in 1769 James Watt made the first that worked efficiently.

During the first decades of the nineteenth century, inventors tried mounting steam engines on carts, linking pistons and wheels to make a machine that moved under its own power—a "locomotive" engine. For centuries wagons rolling on wooden tracks had been used in mines. Their wheels had flanges—raised inside edges—to keep the carts on the rails. In the 1700s this idea had been extended to tramways with iron rails for horse-drawn wagons. When a steam-powered wagon with flanged wheels was mounted onto a tramway, railroad technology was born.

STEPHENSON'S LOCOMOTION NO. 1,
1825

TREVITHICK'S ENGINE,
1804

STEPHENSON'S ROCKET, 1829

EARLY LOCOMOTIVES

In 1804 Englishman Richard Trevithick built the first steam engine to run on a railway, but his machine was too heavy for the tracks and never really used. The most successful of the early locomotive engines were built by George Stephenson, who was chief mechanic of a coal mine. He started experimenting in 1813, constantly refining his ideas in one design after another until he produced the first truly reliable locomotive and the tracks to support it. He was joined in business by his son, Robert, and together they built the world's first public railroad, the Stockton & Darlington line. Authorized by an act of Parliament in 1821, the line was first intended as a tramway for horse-drawn wagons hauling coal from the mines to a terminal on the sea—a distance of about eight miles. But the Stephensons convinced the investors that one of their engines could do the work of fifty horses, so they were given the job of building the entire railway and supplying the locomotives.

On September 27, 1825, the Stockton & Darlington ran for the first time, and huge crowds assembled along the route to witness the spectacle. Out in front rode a horseman carrying a flag. Chugging and puffing its way behind was Locomotion No. 1, the latest of George Stephenson's steam engines. Connected directly to the locomotive was its "tender," a special car for carrying the fuel—a barrel of water for the boiler and a supply of coal for the firebox. The tender was followed by six cars full of coal. Then came a passenger coach for the company directors, followed by twenty-one open wagons fitted with temporary seats for about 450 adventurous passengers. After a while the horseman got out of the way, Stephenson opened the throttle, and Locomotion No. 1 reached a speed of about fifteen miles per hour. When the world's first public railroad train reached Stockton, it was greeted by church bells, a thundering cannon, and a brass band.

In spite of the successful demonstration, the Stockton & Darlington line was still basically a train for hauling coal. But in 1830, after several years of construction, the Liverpool & Manchester Railway opened for business. This train carried passengers and freight for a distance of almost forty miles between two major cities in England, and is regarded as the first real railroad. Massive bridges were built to carry the rails over gorges, and deep cuts for the tracks were made through rugged terrain. The Stephensons' newest locomotive won a competition to provide the service. It was called Rocket, and could reach a speed of thirty-five miles per hour. Now it was possible for large numbers of people to go quickly from one place to another and for any kind of goods to be transported economically and swiftly. Railroad technology was poised to transform the world.

RAILROAD MANIA

All of these exciting events in England were followed closely in America. Curious engineers went abroad to see the new technology, and ambitious businessmen began starting up railroad companies even before they had reliable locomotives. Organized in 1827, the Baltimore & Ohio Railroad was the first public railroad to be chartered in the United States, but it was soon followed by others. Locomotives imported from England became the prototypes for the first American-made engines. One of the best known was built by inventor Peter Cooper in 1830. It was very small, not much more than a boiler on wheels, and was christened Tom Thumb. After its first successful run, Cooper was challenged to race a horse-drawn carriage. The little locomotive kept a smart lead until its steam engine failed, and the horse famously won. But the iron horse would be the ultimate victor, and eventually technology left the horse behind as a means of transportaion.

As more businessmen recognized the advantages of railroads for commerce, scores of railway companies were chartered and machine shops began manufacturing locomotives. On Christmas Day in 1830, the South Carolina Canal and Rail Road Company of Charleston, its locomotives built in New York, carried the first passengers in America for a short ride. The new method of transportation spread like wildfire. By 1840 there were 1,300 miles of rails in England and more than 2,800 miles in the eastern part of America. The first great wave of railroad building was under way.

Engineers constantly made improvements and added features to their locomotives. Some of the earliest engines had a single pair of driving wheels attached directly to the piston rods. The other wheels were for support and were unpowered. But by coupling identical wheels together on each side of the engine by means of connecting rods, engineers increased the number of driving wheels and the traction they produced. Boilers and fireboxes of cast iron were made larger, designed to generate more power. Another important innovation was the pivoting "bogie," a truck with small nondriving wheels placed under the very front of the locomotive for support and to guide it around curves. Wedge-shaped devices known as pilots were attached to the front of the bogies to push aside debris and even animals from the tracks. They came to be called "cowcatchers." Huge smokestacks had internal arresters for capturing stray sparks and cinders, and gas lanterns, steam whistles, and bells contributed to safety. Enclosed engine cabs were added to protect the engineer and accompanying fireman from the weather. With all of its improvements and additions, this powerful, enlarged type of locomotive was in wide use in the United States by the 1850s. Called the "American Standard," it was the workhorse of the nineteenth-century American railroad industry. Over the next decades many thousands of them were built.

Railroad engineers took great pride in their magnificent machines. They decorated their locomotives with bright colors, polished brass trim, ornamental scrollwork, and even painted scenes. As the trains chugged along, belching steam, smoke, cinders, and sparks while their pumping rods turned big powerful wheels, these iron horses seemed almost like living things. Engineers responded by giving their engines romantic names such as Cyclone, Goliath, Hiawatha, Hercules, Hannibal, Lightning, and Stampede. The public was captured by a kind of "railroad mania," and the new technology quickly became part of the fabric of life.

WESTWARD EXPANSION

By the mid-nineteenth century, America was looking westward. California became the thirty-first state in 1850, and other new states were gradually carved out of the western territories. Many people had the foresight to believe that one day there would be a nation of states encompassing the entire width of the North American continent between the Atlantic and Pacific oceans, "from sea to shining sea." This idea was even considered to be the obvious and inevitable will of God—the nation's "manifest destiny." But there was one obstacle—most of the West was wilderness. The vast expanse of the Great Plains and the rugged mountain barriers of the Rockies and the Sierra Nevada made travel extremely difficult and dangerous. It took months to cross the continent overland by wagon or to sail around South America to California. The railroad held the key to America's expansion. The eastern seaboard was linked via railway to the Great Lakes in 1850 and to a little town called Chicago in 1852. In 1856 the first railroad bridge was built across the Mississippi River. By 1860, on the eve of the Civil War and only

thirty years after the first railroad company opened for business in America, there were thirty thousand miles of track in the eastern United States and the railroad was poised at the edge of the Great Plains.

The Civil War was the most terrible conflict in American history, and the railroads played a central role in determining its outcome. When war broke out in 1861, more than two thirds of the nation's railroad lines were in the northern states, giving them an enormous advantage in moving troops, supplies, and weapons quickly over hundreds of miles. This marked the first time in history that railroads were part of the arsenal of war, and they were critical to the ultimate victory of the North over the South in 1865.

But even in the midst of the conflict, the idea of manifest destiny was not forgotten. In 1862, while war raged on, President Lincoln signed into law the Pacific Railway Act, which provided funding for a transcontinental railroad line to link California to the eastern states. It was an unprecedented undertaking—constructing a ribbon of iron rails through the wilderness across a distance of about 1,800 miles. The Central Pacific Railroad Company started laying track eastward from Sacramento, California, while the Union Pacific Railroad Company built westward from Omaha, Nebraska, in a race to meet somewhere in the middle. Construction was slow at first, but after the war ended in 1865, the work began in earnest.

The two companies employed thousands of men and draft animals, all organized like armies going into battle. First came the scouts and surveyors, who determined the best way forward, followed by axmen in the mountains for cutting trees. Engineers and construction crews built bridges over gorges and rivers and blasted tunnels and deep cuts through rugged mountain

terrain. Next came the location men, who staked out the exact path of the rails, followed by crews who prepared the roadbed to receive the tracks. Finally there were the "iron men," tracklayers who actually put down the rails. In addition to the gangs of workers who constructed the railroad, there were also complete support crews of carpenters, mechanics, blacksmiths, and even office workers, such as telegraph operators for communication with the outside world and bookkeepers for keeping track of everything. Teams of cooks were employed to feed the thousands of men. While crews of hunters and trappers provided some game, most other supplies and provisions had to be brought in enormous quantities to the front lines by rail or wagon train. Cowboys drove herds of cattle for a constant supply of fresh beef.

Railroad equipment such as ties, rails, and spikes were brought by trains that shuttled back and forth from California or Nebraska to the front lines on the new rails that stretched behind the teams of iron men. The actual laying of track was organized in a kind of assembly line, with each man doing a particular task over and over. This process became so efficient that on a good day several miles could be laid. The all-time record was an astonishing ten miles of track laid in one day—nearly a mile every hour! On the Union Pacific portion of the line, most of the unskilled and dangerous work was done by Irish immigrants, newly arrived from Europe and desperately in need of work, and by soldiers recently released from service during the Civil War. The Central Pacific employed hundreds of Chinese workers, recruited from San Francisco's Chinatown and also brought all the way from China just to work on the railroad.

Native Americans who lived in the path of the railroad watched all of this activity with alarm. Already forced onto reservations, they knew that their territories were shrinking and that their way of life was gradually being destroyed. Sometimes bands of braves mounted raids against the

railroad in a vain attempt to slow the invasion, and in response military escorts were assigned to provide protection for the railroad workers.

The two railroad lines finally met to form one at a little place called Promontory, Utah. On May 10, 1869, the Central Pacific's Jupiter and the Union Pacific's No. 119, two American Standard locomotives, faced each other at Promontory, separated only by the length of one rail. After a ceremony with speeches and congratulations all around, a large, boisterous crowd watched as the last few spikes, including a ceremonial one made of solid gold, were tapped into a polished laurel wood tie by railroad officials. Then the two great machines, hissing steam, inched forward and gently touched pilots. The transcontinental railroad was complete. It was an amazing epic achievement, one of the great technological feats of the nineteenth century.

THE GREAT AGE OF STEAM

In the decades following the meeting of the rails at Promontory, the eastern United States became more and more industrialized, the West was gradually settled, and the railroads of America kept growing. By 1890 there were several different transcontinental lines and a total of more than 163,000 miles of track in the nation. Everywhere the trains went, business followed and new towns and cities prospered, while existing towns unlucky enough to be bypassed by the railroad shriveled and died. Business on a scale never before imagined became possible because of the railroad. Bold and aggressive men took advantage of the opportunities and became immensely wealthy. People began to move around more than ever before. Those with more leisure time began to travel for pleasure. The railroad stood at the center of American life and culture.

THE TRANSC
RAIL

MEETING OT

PROMONTORY, UTA

JUPITER

But travel by rail was not without its hazards. During this period, accidents were fairly common because of higher speeds, faulty equipment, primitive signaling practices, and badly constructed tracks. Sometimes boilers exploded, bridges collapsed, or iron rails broke. When a train crashed, wooden coaches would smash and then catch fire from overturned oil lamps or coal stoves. A train wreck was a new and terrifying kind of disaster in which large numbers of people could be killed or maimed, and nineteenth-century America reacted in horror. Famous wrecks were memorialized in lurid newspaper articles, sad poems, and doleful ballads, such as "The Wreck of the Old 97":

> He was going down grade, making ninety miles an hour
> When his whistle broke into a scream.
> (Wooo! Wooo!)
> He was found in the wreck with his hand on the throttle,
> And a-scalded to death by the steam.

One of the most horrible accidents occurred in Ashtabula, Ohio, in 1876, when a bridge collapsed under the Pacific Express one winter night. The train plunged eighty feet into the frozen creek below. As the wooden cars crashed, they burst into flame, and the wreckage became a raging inferno in which more than eighty people died. It was the worst railroad accident to that date.

But as the decades passed, technology improved and so did safety. The most critical innovation was the use of steel, which was being mass produced by the 1880s. Iron bridges, rails,

and locomotives were gradually replaced by ones made of the much harder and more durable metal, and by the end of the century, most lines were rolling on steel. Before the invention of air brakes, brakemen had to go from the top of one train car to the next in any kind of weather, turning the brake wheel atop each one by hand—an incredibly difficult and hazardous job. Now a train could be slowed and stopped from the engine cab, and Congress made air brakes mandatory for all trains in 1893. Better coupling devices for connecting cars and the adoption of standard signaling systems and electric lighting in the 1880s also contributed to greater safety. In turn, all of these innovations made it possible to build much larger, heavier, and faster trains.

At the turn of the twentieth century, the railroad industry was by far the biggest and most important business in America. The entire nation was stitched together by a vast system of rails, and that network was still expanding. When the system reached its peak in 1918, there were nearly 250,000 miles of railroad track in the United States. The railroad station was the center of almost every town and city. For small towns the depot was their connection to the outside world. As one railroad enthusiast put it, "News, mail, Sears Roebuck catalogues, sewing machines, strangers, relatives, new schoolteachers, scandal, delight, the circus—all came to town on the train." In medium-size cities the railroad station was a symbol of civic pride and prosperity, and its architecture reflected that idea. It might take the form of a turreted castle, an Italian palazzo, or a Roman temple, fronting a big glass and iron train shed. But in the biggest cities, the station was called a terminal—the final destination. The grandest of them were constructed after the turn of the century to replace smaller structures, and they are among the greatest public buildings ever built in America. When it opened in Washington DC in 1907, Union Station was one of the largest structures in the nation. Its entrance still faces the Capitol Building like a stately

triumphal arch. New York's Grand Central Terminal was built between 1903 and 1913, with 123 tracks on two levels, and 48 boarding platforms. The great public room, the Main Concourse, is a vast, cavernous space with a beautiful blue-green vaulted ceiling painted with the constellations of the zodiac, and its famous clock in the center helps keep travelers on time. A few blocks away in New York City, Pennsylvania Station was even grander. Finished in 1910, it covered twenty-eight acres, and was designed in the opulent style of the Baths of Caracalla in ancient Rome. It was simply magnificent, and when it was unfortunately torn down in 1963 and replaced by the post office, the *New York Times* commented that we will "be judged not by the monuments we build, but by those we have destroyed."

The turn of the century also brought with it two very important new inventions—the automobile and the airplane. But in the beginning their technologies were relatively crude and undeveloped, particularly when compared to the steam locomotive, which by now was a very powerful, complex, and sophisticated machine. In 1900 there were forty thousand locomotives in use and more being built every year—6,300 new engines were ordered in 1905 alone. The new generation of locomotives dwarfed the old American Standard. Now made of steel, boilers and fireboxes could be much larger and longer to generate more power. Bigger engines could haul heavier loads, so they needed more driving wheels for support and traction. These locomotives were nearly twice the length of an American Standard and could have as many as twelve driving wheels—six on each side. Anything bigger was too long for rounding curves. Designers were able to overcome this problem by building "articulated" locomotives with two engines mounted under a single boiler, suspended independently for taking curves. As they got larger and larger, locomotives were more powerful and able to pull greater tonnage. The technology was constantly evolving.

The experience of travel evolved as well. The first passenger cars way back in the 1830s were merely stagecoaches with flanged wheels to keep them on track, and soon a standard type of passenger coach with rows of seats was adopted in America. But until the Civil War era, cars were dark, dirty, and cramped. As long-distance travel became more common, the railroads recognized the need for greater comfort. In 1867 George Pullman started a company to make sleeping cars, with upper berths that folded and seat cushions that extended to make lower berths. He also built dining cars like tiny restaurants to provide meals that could be enjoyed while watching the scenery pass by. There were parlor cars, decorated with polished woodwork and comfortable upholstered furniture, and smoking cars for gentlemen. Observation cars had large windows for taking in the view. The extremely wealthy and captains of industry commissioned opulent private cars, lavishly decorated and equipped with every amenity. Travel for those who could afford it was turned from a difficult experience into a pleasure.

In the 1920s and '30s, express passenger trains that ran between the major cities set the standard for luxury. They provided modern and efficient Pullman sleeping cars and dining cars with starched white linen, crystal and silver, and small bouquets of fresh flowers in vases. The porters and waiters attended a special school where they learned "such niceties as how to drive a fly from a car, how to fold linen, and how to wake up their charges (a shake on the curtains from without—never a knock or a word)." Trains were comfortable and glamorous at a time when travel by car was limited, since the highway system was primitive, and commercial flight was just beginning. These "hotels on rails" were pulled by enormous, powerful, and very fast locomotives. To suggest great speed, some designers even covered the open machinery of their express locomotives with sculpted steel hoods, streamlined to look sleek and modern. The train was the way to go.

COMPETITION

Steam is not the only way to power a locomotive. As early as the mid-1890s, single-car locomotives were developed, with relatively small electric motors that turned the wheels. Electricity for this type of locomotive is usually provided by a network of overhead power lines installed above the tracks, but sometimes it is supplied by an extra rail, as in the underground subway system of New York. Building an electric system is expensive, but the trains are easy to maintain and run cleanly because they produce no smoke or steam. This makes electricity ideal for short rail lines, and since the turn of the twentieth century, electric locomotives have been used in American cities and towns for public transportation. Today many passenger trains around the world are electrically powered.

Another competitor for steam locomotion is the diesel engine. First invented in the 1890s, as a type of internal combustion engine that uses oil for fuel, the diesel eventually was adapted to big locomotives in the late 1930s by combining a diesel motor with electric power. In a diesel-electric, the diesel engine turns a generator, which makes electricity for powering the motors that actually turn the wheels. Steam locomotives require constant servicing and repair, and they must pull a heavy tender car that carries their fuel of water and coal. Diesels are more expensive to build than steam engines but are cheaper to maintain in the end. They are much more efficient to operate because they are more durable, they run faster, they require a smaller crew, and they can go much farther before having to refuel their oil tanks. Diesel-electric locomotives were widely adopted first for passenger lines, but during the 1940s and '50s, diesels gradually replaced steam engines on freight trains as well.

World War II was the last hurrah for steam locomotives in America. As the nation's industries geared up for war, almost everything produced ran on the rails. Some of the biggest locomotives ever built were constructed during these years. One of the largest was called "Big Boy." Twenty-five of these were made from 1941 to 1944 for hauling heavy freight. With two engines and sixteen driving wheels, Big Boy was an articulated locomotive capable of pulling a 160-car train at a top speed of eighty miles per hour. It weighed six hundred tons, and was over sixteen feet tall and 132 feet long, including its tender. Truly gargantuan, Big Boy represented the pinnacle of steam technology. But when the war was over in 1945, it was clear that the days of steam were numbered in America—diesels were simply more efficient. Since 1830, about 175,000 steam locomotives had been made, but now the machine that had changed the world was becoming obsolete. The last commercial steam locomotive was built in 1949. For the next ten years or so, the steam engines that remained in service were gradually phased out and replaced by diesels. After more than one hundred years, the Age of Steam was over.

The railroads themselves were also facing stiff competition. By midcentury the automobile and airplane were mature technologies. In 1916, 98 percent of all freight and passenger travel in America was by rail. But by the 1950s, most families owned a car and the Interstate Highway System was under construction. Soon America was bound together by good highways as well as rails, and more and more people took to the road instead of taking the train. The interstates made it possible for long-haul diesel trucks to carry heavy freight, while commercial air travel also exploded during the '50s and '60s, cutting more deeply into the railroad's business. Why spend a few days crossing the country when it could be done in a few hours?

In only a couple of decades the passenger railroad business shrank to a fraction of what it had been. In 1950, out of a total of 225,000 track miles, 147,500 were used for passenger trains; by 1970 only about 42,000 miles were. Today only the big cities of the northeast, midwest, and California have any real passenger rail traffic between them. In New York City scores of commuter trains and the famous subway system carry millions of passengers every day. But New York is unique—only a handful of other American cities have commuter rail lines. There are still a few long-distance passenger trains, which cater mainly to tourists who want the experience of travel by rail. Otherwise American railroads now carry only freight.

But the colorful past is kept alive by railroad enthusiasts, from kids who love model trains to people who preserve, restore, and maintain antique locomotives that have survived the great age of railroading. Some of these relics are now used as exhibits in museums, and others are in active service, carrying tourists on excursions.

BACK TO THE FUTURE

The decline of railroads is purely an American phenomonon. Across the rest of the globe, the railroad has remained a vital and preferred means of travel. In some developing countries, steam locomotives are still used for their mechanical reliability and because they are fueled only by water and coal or wood. And there remain great epic trips to be made by rail. People can travel on trains while spending their time relaxing in comfort, eating great food, and viewing impressive scenery. For example, the Trans-Canada Rail Journey between Toronto and Vancouver passes through the rugged Canadian Rockies, where travelers can view some of the most splendid

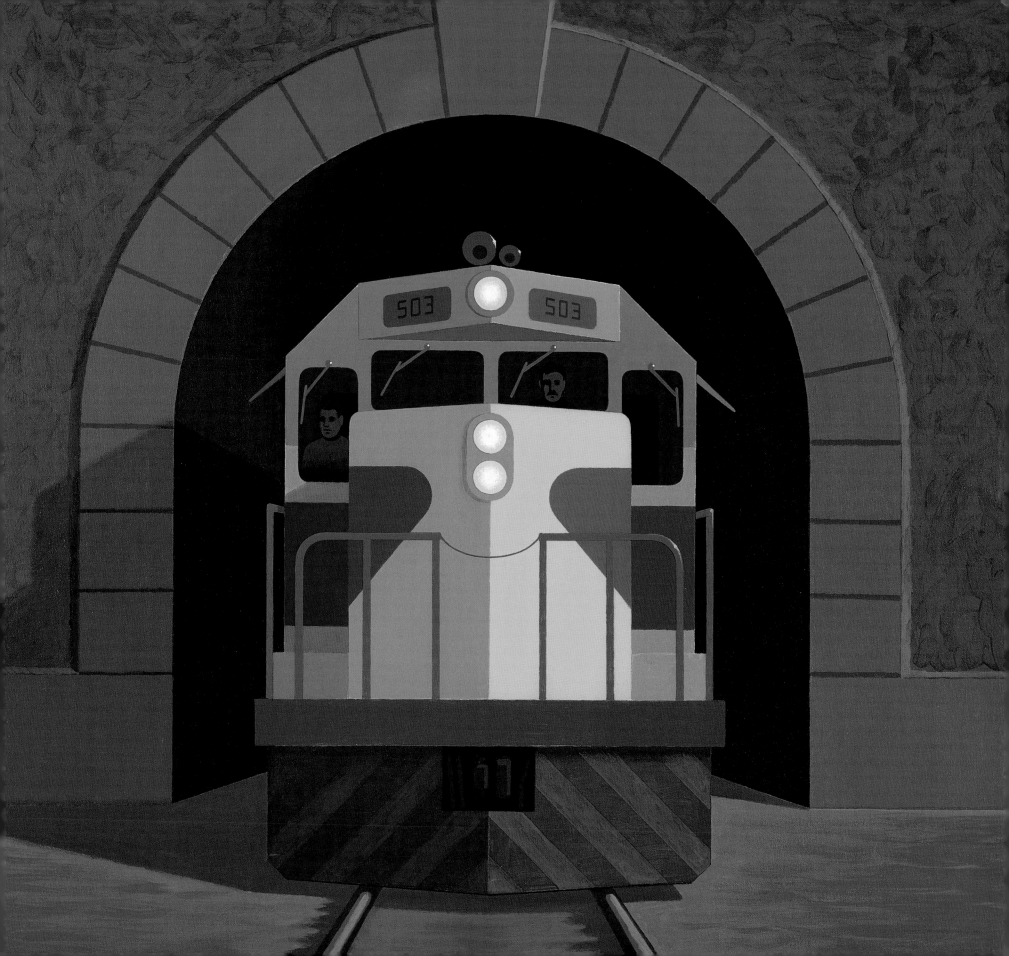

scenery in the world from the line's gleaming stainless-steel domed observation cars. Or there is South Africa's posh Blue Train from Cape Town to Pretoria. Renowned for its deluxe service, the Blue Train offers a side excursion to the spectacular Victoria Falls, one of the largest waterfalls on earth. But perhaps the most famous of all the great rail journeys is the fabulous Orient Express, which once ran on several different lines from Paris through the heart of Europe to exotic Istanbul in Turkey. Now much diminished, the Orient Express used to be a vital link between Western and Eastern cultures and was patronized by royalty, heads of state, and prominent people from the worlds of society and business. Often used as a setting for books and movies, the Orient Express continues to be celebrated for its aura of old-world glamour, mystery, and intrigue. People today don't necessarily take these classic train trips to reach a destination, but to leave their daily lives behind by experiencing the romance of a journey by railroad in the grand tradition, to feel the rhythm of the landscape as it passes by, and to encounter a larger world by following the compelling blast of a train whistle—the haunting, wistful sound that still calls us to places far away.

Meanwhile, Asian and European designers continue to take railway technology into the future with high-speed trains. Japan and the nations of Europe have superb state-supported railways that are well maintained and constantly upgraded. In these countries, with their comprehensive public transportation systems, train travel is a way of life. The first truly high-speed locomotives were Japanese electric bullet trains, with service inaugurated in 1964. Fast, clean, and comfortable, today's bullet trains cruise at speeds approaching two hundred miles per hour. Fleets of these beautiful, futuristic-looking trains connect the cities of Japan with the fastest point-to-point service of any rail line in the world.

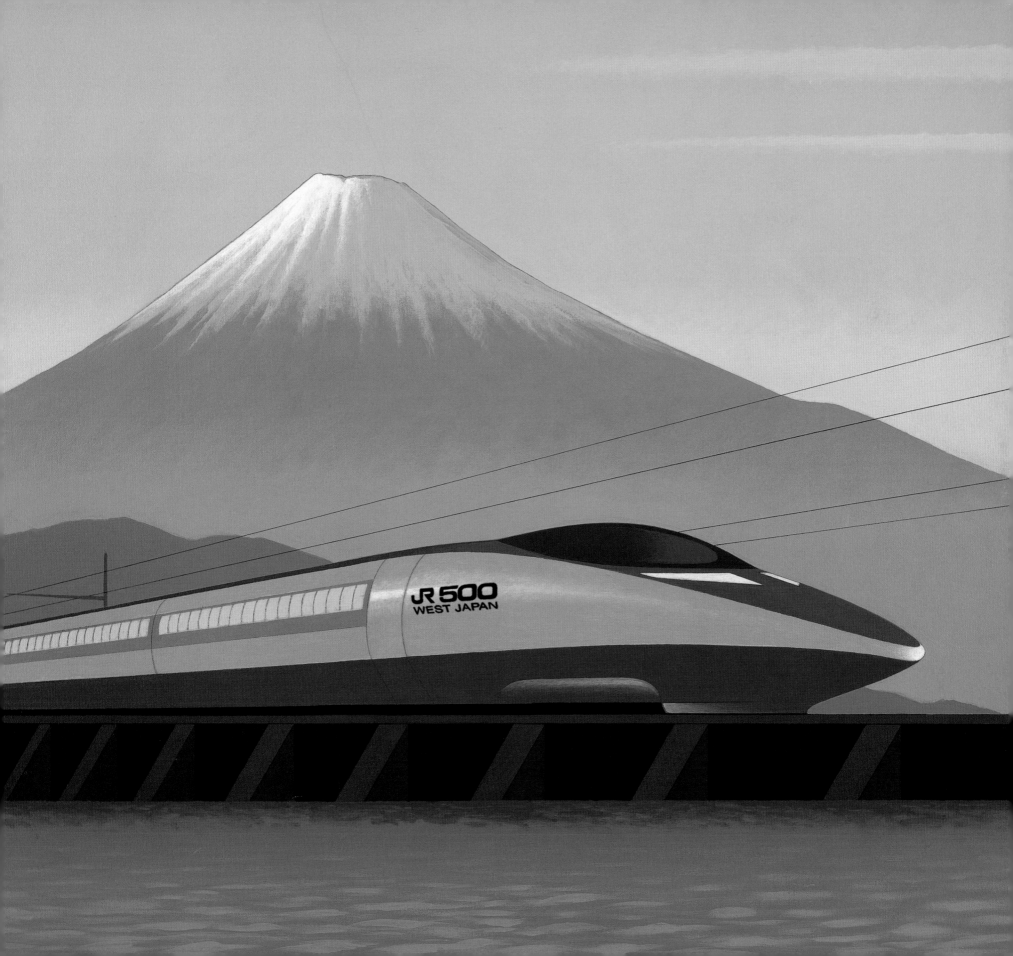

The latest cutting-edge technology in ultra-high-speed trains is "maglev," or magnetic levitation. It sounds like science fiction, but a maglev train actually floats propelled by magnetic forces over a guideway. It can reach speeds of more than three hundred miles per hour. Because the trains don't use existing rails, the entire system must be built from scratch and is very expensive. The technology has been used so far only for experimental short lines in Germany, England, Japan, and China, but the potential is enormous. Long-distance maglev express trains may someday achieve the speeds of aircraft.

Two hundred years after the Industrial Revolution, we now live in a new world with unprecedented challenges for mankind. The chronic energy problem and the reality of global warming are finally forcing us to make serious changes in the way we utilize our resources in the twenty-first century. Transportation accounts for much of our energy use and pollution, but electric and diesel trains are relatively energy-efficient means of transportation and are many times more efficient than automobiles or airplanes. Because of this, there has been renewed interest in upgrading American railroads in the past few years by investing in new technology and building more rapid-transit systems. Modern America was built by the railroads, and the railroad once stood at the center of American life. Although forty years ago it seemed that trains were going the way of the covered wagon, today the railroad may offer us a highway into the future.

It all starts by building a fire. Coal or wood is burned in the firebox to heat an array of tubes in an enclosed boiler partially filled with water. When the water boils, steam collects in the steam dome, and as the pressure builds the engineer opens the throttle, allowing the steam to enter the steam pipe. This long pipe feeds the compressed steam into the cylinder, where the pressure pushes the piston first one way and then the other, by means of an ingenious alternating system

① ENGINE CAB   ④ BOILER AND TUBES   ⑦ CYLINDER

② THROTTLE   ⑤ STEAM DOME   ⑧ PISTON

③ FIREBOX   ⑥ STEAM PIPE   ⑨ SYSTEM OF VALVES

of valves. The piston is connected to one wheel by the piston rod. Connecting rods attach this wheel to the other driving wheels, and as the piston moves back and forth, the wheels rotate together, moving the locomotive. The used steam exhausts up the blast pipe, helping to draw the smoke from the fire up and out of the smokestack.

⑩ PISTON ROD   ⑬ SMOKE BOX   ⑯ BOGIE

⑪ CONNECTING RODS   ⑭ BLAST PIPE   ⑰ SUPPORTING WHEELS

⑫ DRIVING WHEELS   ⑮ SMOKESTACK   ⑱ PILOT

SOURCES

Chant, Christopher. *The World's Railroads: The History and Development of Rail Transport.* Edison, New Jersey: Chartwell Books, 2002.

Halberstadt, Hans and April. *Great American Train Stations: Classic Terminals and Depots.* New York: Barnes and Noble, 1997.

Jensen, Oliver. *The American Heritage History of Railroads in America.* New York: American Heritage Publishing, 1975.

Nock, O. S., ed. *Encyclopedia of Railroads.* New York: Galahad Books, 1977.

Ross, David, and Brian Solomon. *The Heritage of North American Trains: Steam, Diesel, and Electric Locomotives from Pioneer Days to Modern Times.* New York: New Line Books, 2006.

Shipman, Roy J., ed. *High Point: A Pictorial History.* High Point, North Carolina: Hall Printing, 1983.

Welsh, Joe, with Jim Boyd and William F. Howes Jr. *The American Railroad: Working for the Nation.* St. Paul, Minnesota: MBI, 2006.

For my friends Gail, Michael, Tim, Dick, and Kim

Atheneum Books for Young Readers
An imprint of Simon & Schuster Children's Publishing Division
1230 Avenue of the Americas, New York, New York 10020
Copyright © 2009 by Lynn Curlee
All rights reserved, including the right of reproduction in whole or in part in any form.
Book design by Krista Vossen
The text for this book is set in Aldus.
The illustrations for this book are rendered in acrylic on canvas.
Mr. Curlee would like to thank Ed Peterson for photographing the paintings.
Manufactured in China
First Edition
2 4 6 8 10 9 7 5 3 1
Library of Congress Cataloging-in-Publication Data
Curlee, Lynn.
Trains / Lynn Curlee. — 1st ed.
p. cm.
ISBN: 978-1-4169-4848-3
1. Railroad—History—Juvenile literature. I. Title.
HE1021.C87 2010
385.09—dc22
2007040425